TWO MILLENNIA OF CHURCH HISTORY

by Renald Showers

Copyright © 1998 by The Friends of Israel Gospel Ministry, Inc.
Bellmawr, NJ 08099

Fifth Printing 2016

ISBN 0-915540-67-3

Cover/layout by Thomas E. Williams.

Visit our website at *www.foi.org*

About Church History

O ver two thousand years have transpired since Jesus Christ, the Son of God, was born in the land of Israel. While He was here He said, "I will build my church" (Mt. 16:18). Through His death on the cross for the sins of the world, burial in a tomb, and bodily resurrection three days after his death, Jesus enabled the church to be born and to be built (Eph. 2:13-22). The church began on the Day of Pentecost, ten days after the Lord Jesus ascended to God the Father in heaven (Acts 1-2).

For almost two thousand years since its birth the church has been in the process of being built. Church history is the record of that construction. It is an important record because it reveals what happens when the church is led in the right direction, and what results when it is led astray.

Tragically, the church is often led in wrong directions because the majority of Christians don't know its history. For the sake of the church it is imperative that such lack of knowledge be corrected. To that end, an overview of the two millennia of the church's history has been prepared. It is presented with the hope that it will help to make a difference for the benefit of the church and the glory of Jesus Christ, its Head (Eph. 1:20-23).

Renald E. Showers

Ancient
Church History

THE APOSTOLIC CHURCH
(EARLY 30s–100 A.D.)

*E*arly Beginnings. The church begins on Pentecost in the early 30s A.D. (Acts 2). Membership is entirely Jewish for several years, and the church is led by Jewish apostles. Deacons are appointed to serve the church.

Early Persecution. Jewish unbelievers persecute Jewish believers, led by Saul of Tarsus, a Pharisee. The Sanhedrin kills Stephen, a Jewish deacon.

Early Expansion. Samaritans and the Ethiopian eunuch believe in Christ and enter the church through the preaching of Philip, a Jewish deacon. Saul of Tarsus comes to faith in Christ as a result of the resurrected, glorified Christ appearing to him. Saul becomes Paul, a Jewish apostle. Gentiles believe in Christ and enter the church through the preaching of Peter, a Jewish apostle.

More Persecution. Herod Agrippa I persecutes the apostles; the apostle James is killed.

The Antioch Church. Jewish believers bring the gospel to Gentiles in Antioch of Syria. The first predominantly Gentile church is established here. In Antioch believers are first called *Christians*. The Antioch church sends Paul and Barnabas as Jewish missionaries on their first missionary journey to Cyprus, Pamphylia, Pisidia, and Lycaonia. Many Gentiles become believers. Paul and Barnabas appoint elders to lead each new church.

The First Church Council. The first church council meets in Jerusalem. Decision: Gentiles can be saved and enter the church as Gentiles; they do not have to become Jews.

Later Expansion. Paul and Barnabas go on separate missionary journeys. On his second journey, Paul plants churches in seven key cities and carries the gospel to Europe.

On his third, Paul builds an excellent church in Ephesus and plants the gospel in all of Asia Minor. Then he is held prisoner for about five years. After his release he takes a fourth journey, possibly to Spain, then is imprisoned again.

The Beginning of Roman Persecution. Emperor Nero begins the Roman persecution of the church in 64 A.D. Later he murders the apostles Peter and Paul.

The Destruction of Jerusalem. Jewish Christians do not participate in the Jewish War against Rome. They cross the Jordan River and settle in Pella, escaping the horrors of the Roman siege and destruction of Jerusalem and the Second (Herod's) Temple in 70 A.D.

More Roman Persecution. Emperor Domitian persecutes the church extensively (81 - 96 A.D.). The apostle John is exiled to the Island of Patmos, where he receives and writes the Revelation of Jesus Christ.

The Writing of the New Testament. The New Testament is written from the mid-40s to the mid-90s A.D. Revelation is written last.

The Church at the End of the Apostolic Age. The Apostolic Age ends when the last

apostle, John, dies around 100 A.D. By now the church is strong, aggressive, and growing. Local churches exist in every major city from Italy in the west (including, perhaps, Spain and Britain) to the Tigris-Euphrates Rivers in the east, from the Black Sea in the north to North Africa in the south. Believers come from every class but mostly from poor and slave classes. Yet all are equal in the church and hold positions of leadership. Baptism and communion are conducted for believers only. Sunday gradually replaces the Sabbath as the day of worship. Some churches observe one Sunday a year as the anniversary of Christ's resurrection. Moral standards are high, but spiritual life is lower than desired.

THE PERSECUTED CHURCH
(100–313 A.D.)

Spontaneous Roman Persecution. From 100 to approximately 250 A.D. Roman persecution erupts in certain localities. Many Christians become martyrs.

Planned Roman Persecution. From approximately 250 to 311 A.D. government persecution is planned and vigorous. Officials throughout the empire are ordered to arrest Christians and give them an ultimatum: Deny your faith in Jesus Christ, or die. It becomes official policy to destroy Christianity. Vast numbers of Christians refuse to deny Jesus and become martyrs, often as public entertainment in large arenas. Yet the church grows stronger and expands throughout the empire.

Heresies and Divisive Issues. During the persecution, the church faces the heresies of legalism, Gnosticism, Manicheanism, Neo-Platonism, Montanism, and Monarchianism. It also contends with two major, divisive issues: When should Easter be celebrated, and what should be done with professing Christians who deny their faith to escape persecution?

Official End of Roman Persecution. In 311 A.D. Emperor Galerius issues the Edict of Toleration, commanding that Christians be tolerated. This officially ends the Roman persecution. In 313 A.D. Emperor Constantine issues the Edict of Milan, granting Christians total freedom. Now they may meet freely for worship and openly propagate their faith.

Development of Views and Practices. During the persecution, the title *Catholic* (meaning "universal") is applied to the organized church throughout the Roman Empire. Some leaders begin advocating the concepts of apostolic succession (the idea that the apostles' authority is passed to key church leaders) and the primacy of Peter (the idea that Peter was the foremost apostle). Some leaders in the eastern segment of the church develop the allegorical (as opposed to literal) method of interpreting the Bible. This method and the influence of Greek philosophy cause some leaders to reject and attack chiliasm (the view known today as *Premillennialism*)—the original eschatological position of the church. Some leaders begin writing and preaching anti-Semitic concepts. A cycle of feast days develop: Easter is observed universally by 300 A.D., some observe Christ's birthday on January 6, and some begin the practice of Lent. The fish becomes a symbol of Christianity. Some begin baptizing infants. Construction of church buildings begins in the early 300s. Some begin to regard communion as a sacrifice. Some begin praying to dead saints.

Development of Organization. Around 125 A.D. local assemblies begin elevating one elder in authority over others. He is called the monarchal (ruling) bishop of the local church. These bishops are equal in authority with each other. By the 200s, local churches throughout the Roman Empire are grouped into divisions paralleling the diocesan political divisions of the empire. The bishop of the largest local assembly in the largest city of each church diocese receives the title of metropolitan bishop and has authority over the other bishops in his diocese. By 313 A.D. the church is well organized and large (perhaps some sixty million members).

THE STATE CHURCH (313–590 A.D.)

Union of Church and State. 324 A.D.—Emperor Constantine decrees Christianity the state religion of the Roman Empire and declares himself to be a Christian. 380 A.D.—Emperor Theodosius I makes Christianity the sole religion allowed within the empire. Pagan religions are outlawed, and there is complete union of church and state.

Missionary Activity. Early 300s A.D.—Celts of Britain become true believers in Jesus before the Angles and Saxons invade. 432-461 A.D.—Ireland converts to Celtic Christianity through the missionary work of Patrick, a British, Celtic Christian. By 496 A.D. the king of the Franks and his people adopt Christianity. Columba, an Irish Christian, leads in the evangelization of Scotland.

Church Councils and Theological Disputes. From 313 to 590 A.D. the church faces theological disputes concerning the person of Jesus Christ, the person of the Holy Spirit, the nature of man, and how man is saved. Several church councils convene to examine and settle these issues.

Development of Organized Monasticism. Some individuals pursue a monastic lifestyle through isolation. Eventually monasteries are built, where monks worship and live together apart from society. The first monastery is built on an island in the Nile River in 340 A.D. In the early 500s the first monastic order, the Benedictine Order, is established under Benedict's Rule of poverty, chastity, and obedience.

Emergence of Roman Catholicism. Between 313 and 590 A.D. the organized church changes from the Catholic church (with each bishop equal) to the Roman Catholic Church (with the Roman bishop as first among equals). Bishops of the church in Rome claim their church was founded by the apostles Peter and Paul, that Peter was its first bishop, that Christ appointed Peter to be His vicar on earth, and that the bishops of Rome inherit this vicarship of Christ by apostolic succession from Peter. By 590 A.D. these claims are accepted in the western half of the organized church. In 445 A.D. the Roman emperor officially recognizes the primacy of the Roman bishops. Leo I (440-461 A.D.) is the first Roman bishop to assume the title of *papas* ("pope"). He claims judicial authority for the Roman church over the entire church. When the western half of the Roman Empire falls in 476 A.D., the Roman church provides leadership and stability for Western Europe.

Development of Views and Practices. The following concepts develop between 313 and 590 A.D: purgatory and baptismal regeneration; veneration of angels, saints, relics, statues, and pictures; the system of seven sacraments; the observance of Christ's birth on December 25; more holy days; Sunday as an official day of rest and worship; antiphonal singing; acceptance of infant baptism; communion as a sacrifice; pilgrimages for penitential and thanksgiving purposes; the building of magnificent church buildings. Veneration of Mary begins. She is called "the mother of God" and "the queen of heaven"; eternal virginity and sinlessness are ascribed to her; prayers are offered to her; she is made the head of all saints and is said to have ascended bodily into heaven. Augustine popularizes the amillennial view of eschatology, which strips Israel of future blessing.

Condition of the Church. The union of church and state makes the organized church rich. It begins adopting the world's standards and becomes polluted with pagans, who find it politically and socially expedient to associate with local churches. They introduce pagan beliefs and practices into the organized church.

Medieval
Church History

THE LATIN-TEUTONIC CHURCH (590–800 A.D.)

*P*apal Authority and Influence. Gregory I, bishop of Rome (590-604 A.D.), becomes the first real pope in the sense of authority and influence. He gains control over the churches of Gaul, Spain, Belgium, Britain, Africa, and Italy by sending Roman missionaries there and handpicking the bishops. He befriends the emperor of the eastern half of the Roman Empire, who calls him "head of all the churches." He makes the Roman church the wealthiest and the virtual political ruler over the province around Rome. He helps develop the concepts of purgatory, transubstantiation, and the worship of saints;

claims that church tradition equals the authority of the Bible; and strongly supports monasticism.

Missionary Activity. Pope Gregory sends Roman missionaries to southern England to convert the Anglo-Saxons to the Roman brand of Christianity. The Celtic Christians oppose this intrusion so strongly that the Anglo-Saxon king convenes a meeting in 664 A.D. to decide which brand of Christianity will be the sole one allowed in England. He chooses Rome because it claims to have the keys to heaven. Other areas convert to Roman Catholicism: the Visigoths in Spain in 589 A.D., Belgium and Holland, the Lombards of southern Italy by 675 A.D., and most of Germany by 718 A.D.

The Impact of Islam. The organized church loses Palestine, Asia Minor, Egypt, and North Africa to Islam. Since Muslims regard all images and pictures as idolatry, the eastern segment of the church changes to reach Muslims for Christianity. After considerable controversy, in 787 A.D. the eastern church decides as follows: Pictures are allowed in worship; most images are abolished; only what the pictures and images represent are to be worshiped. The Roman bishop becomes more powerful because some of his rivals in the East come under Muslim domination or lose much of their domains.

The Donation of Constantine. In the 700s A.D. an official-looking document (*The Donation of Constantine*) appears in Western Europe. It claims that in the 300s, Emperor Constantine gave the bishop of Rome supreme authority over all Europe, even above the emperors. It declares the Roman church supreme over all others and the Roman

bishop the supreme bishop, gives the Roman bishop the emperor's palace in Rome plus the clothing and insignia of the emperor, and moves the capital to Constantinople so as not to interfere with the imperial rights of the Roman bishop in Europe. The Roman church gains great power through this document until it is discovered to be a fraud in the 1400s.

Revival of Western Imperialism. During the late 700s Charlemagne, king of the Franks, amasses the most territory ruled by one man in Western Europe since the fall of the western half of the Roman Empire. On Christmas Day, 800 A.D., the pope crowns Charlemagne "emperor of the Romans." This act revives imperialism in the West, gives birth to the idea that political rulers must receive their crowns from the pope, obligates political rulers to aid the pope when in trouble, and instigates the following new philosophy in Europe: The Kingdom of God has two arms—the spiritual, with the pope over human souls, and the political, with the emperor over human physical life. Thus the pope and emperor are to give each other mutual support. This philosophy sets the stage for conflict between popes and emperors for the rest of the Middle Ages.

THE CORRUPT, DIVIDED CHURCH (800–1054 A.D.)

Papal Corruption. From 867 to 1049 the papacy degenerates to its lowest point. More than 40 persons occupy the papal throne. As various noblemen seize church positions for their sons or relatives, organized Christendom becomes infested with corrupt, immoral bishops and popes who know almost no theology. Several popes are assassinated by their successors. Some have mistresses. One fathers an illegitimate son. Another worships pagan gods and turns the papal palace into a house of prostitution. Another sells the papacy for money. At one time three different men claim to be pope. Pope Leo IX finally ends this corruption in 1049 A.D.

The Holy Roman Empire. Charlemagne dies, and his empire is divided into thirds. Germany becomes dominant. German ruler Otto I rescues Pope John XII from trouble in Italy, and Pope John crowns Otto "emperor of the Holy Roman Empire" in 962 A.D. Central Europe comes under German control.

The Isidorian Decretals. In the mid-800s documents called the *Isidorian Decretals* appear in Europe. They claim to be decrees from Roman bishops since apostolic times. Some are genuine; others are frauds. They claim absolute supremacy of the pope over all church leaders, total freedom of the Roman church from state control, and exempt the clergy from trial in secular courts. Many popes use these decretals to support their claim to power.

Missionary Activity. Denmark, Norway, Sweden, and Iceland become Roman Catholic around 1000 A.D., mainly through the effort of one missionary, Ansgar. Russia, Central Europe, and Eastern Europe convert to Greek or Eastern Orthodox Christianity.

Papal Election. In 1059 A.D. the Roman people lose their right to elect popes. It goes to church leaders called *cardinals*, who hold an electoral meeting called the *College of Cardinals*.

Monastic Reform. By the 900s the Benedictine monasteries are rich and corrupt. A movement to reform them begins in Cluny, France, in 910 A.D. It condemns simony (the buying and selling of church offices) and nepotism (the appointing of relatives to church offices), urges the enforcement of celibacy for clergy, demands the state relinquish all control over the church, and demands that all monks be subject to papal authority. By 950 A.D. this movement becomes a new monastic order, the Cluniac Order.

The Split of 1054 A.D. In 1054 A.D. organized Christendom splits into east and west. Thus begins the formal organization known as the Greek or Eastern Orthodox Church. The western church remains the Roman Catholic Church. Several issues lead to this split: Did the Holy Spirit proceed from the Father and Son or only from the Father? Should clergy be forbidden or required to marry? What type of bread should be used in communion? Should clergy be required to wear beards? When should Easter be observed? Should a weekly fast day be required? Should images and pictures be allowed in worship? Should the patriarch (bishop) of Constantinople be forced to recognize the pope as supreme ruler of the church? In 1054 the pope and patriarch excommunicate each other from the church.

Transubstantiation. In the 830s a French monk, Radbertus, strives to popularize transubstantiation (the concept that the communion bread and wine miraculously change to the flesh and blood of Christ).

THE DOMINATING CHURCH (1054–1305 A.D.)

During this period the Roman Catholic Church dominates all phases of Western European life.

Significant Popes. *Pope Gregory VII* (1073-1085) reforms the clergy, frees the organized church from state control, makes the organized church supreme over the state, claims the pope is God's vice-regent on earth with authority to depose political rulers and release subjects from allegiance to them, and claims the Roman Catholic Church is always free from error. *Pope Innocent III*

(1198-1216) claims that God has committed the whole world to the pope, and the pope can depose political rulers and subject their nations to the interdict (removal of all church ministries to the people until their ruler submits to the pope). He forces the emperor of the Holy Roman Empire and the kings of France and England into submission. He instigates the Fourth Crusade, which persecutes Jews, conquers Constantinople, brings the Eastern Roman Empire (Byzantium) under the pope's rule, and makes him the most powerful man in Europe. He forbids lay people to own Bibles. In 1215 A.D. he convenes the Fourth Lateran Council, which requires celibacy of priests, makes transubstantiation official dogma, and requires confession to a priest at least once a year. *Pope Boniface VIII* (1294-1303) claims salvation does not exist apart from the Roman Catholic Church and submission to the pope.

The Crusades. From 1095 to 1272 nine "Christian" military expeditions go from Western Europe to the East. Most attempt to liberate Palestine from the Muslims. Some persecute the Jewish people and wage war against eastern Christians.

Monastic Reform. By the 1000s the Cluniac Order is wealthy and corrupt. Between 1098 and 1215 new reforms give birth to the Cistercian, Augustinian, Franciscan, and Dominican Orders.

Lay Reform Movements. During the Middle Ages, groups arise that reject the Roman Catholic Church, believing it contrary to the Bible in belief and practice. One such group, the Waldenses, emphasize a personal encounter with Jesus Christ. They believe in religious liberty, in the Bible as the final authority for belief and practice, that everyone should have the Bible in his own language, in two ordinances, and that the dead go immediately to heaven or hell. They reject Roman Catholic miracles, festivals, fasts, orders, offices, transubstantiation, purgatory, and prayers to the dead and saints. In France, they send laymen to preach in French. The pope forbids this, but they refuse to obey him. Beginning in 1184 A.D. the Waldenses endure 400 years of severe persecution. Many are killed, but the group survives. Because they and other lay reform groups base their beliefs on the Bible, the Roman Catholic Synod of Toulouse (1229 A.D.) forbids lay people to have the Bible in their own language.

The Inquisition. To prevent professing Catholics from teaching contrary views or secretly practicing Judaism or Islam, the Roman Catholic Church sets up the Inquisition through the Dominicans and Franciscans. Loyal Catholics are threatened with excommunication for failing to turn in the names of heretics. Papal agents conduct "trials" with no witnesses, accusers, or jury. Thousands are jailed, tortured, or executed for refusing to recant their heresy.

Thomas Aquinas (1226-1274). Aquinas' work, *Summa Theologiae*, becomes the foremost expression of Roman Catholic theology. It claims that Christ and saints store an extra supply of merit in heaven on behalf of sinners on earth. This merit can be put on a sinner's account through the purchase of indulgences. This theology strengthens the view of sacraments as the channels of God's grace.

THE DECLINING CHURCH (1305–1517 A.D.)

Immorality of the Clergy. Many priests father illegitimate children. Some indulge in luxurious living; others devote more time to secular than spiritual matters.

The Babylonian Captivity. From 1309 to 1377 French kings dominate the papacy and move it from Rome to Avignon, France, where it stays for almost seventy years. This period becomes known as the Babylonian Captivity.

The Great Schism. Pope Urban VI mistreats the cardinals who elected him to office in 1378 A.D. They respond by electing Clement VII to replace Urban. Clement moves the papacy back to Avignon, and Urban stays in Rome. Both claim to be the rightful pope. The rivalry splits the religious allegiance of Europe's nations.

Papal Taxation. Political rulers and middle classes begin to resent the many taxes and money-raising schemes the papacy imposes upon their nations.

Rise of Nation-States. Feudalism gives way to nation-states in Europe. People resent the papacy intruding into national affairs, support their rulers in conflicts with the papacy, and begin demanding reform within the Roman Catholic Church.

The Pre-Reformers. Several men try to reform the church to make it follow the New Testament beliefs and practices of the early church. *John Wycliffe* (1324-1384 A.D.) lays the foundation for the Protestant Reformation. A Roman Catholic priest, he criticizes monasticism and the immoral clergy. He rejects papal authority (by naming Christ, not the pope, as head of the church) and rejects transubstantiation (by contending the elements are only symbols of Christ's body and blood). He declares the Bible, not the church, is the sole authority for faith and practice, and he produces the first, complete, English New Testament. *John Huss* (1369-1415), a Roman Catholic priest and administrator at the University of Prague, preaches Wycliffe's views. The pope excommunicates him and demands he appear for trial before a church council. The Holy Roman emperor guarantees him safe conduct, but that guarantee is violated, and Huss is burned at the stake. *Savonarola* (1452-1498), a Dominican monk in Florence, Italy, attacks clergy and papal corruption. He is tortured and hanged.

The Reforming Councils. From 1409 to 1449 a series of church councils meet to reform the Roman Catholic Church. These councils end the Great Schism and try to establish a more democratic church government. The pope crushes this move by setting up a rival council and thus maintains papal authority. The rival council makes the seven sacraments official dogma but fails to reform the Roman Catholic Church, making the Protestant Reformation inevitable.

The Renaissance. Between 1350 and 1650 Western Europe moves from the Middle Ages to modern times due to the Renaissance, which develops along two lines and emphasizes rediscovery of the ancient past. *The Southern or Latin Renaissance* (primarily in Italy) focuses on the classical knowledge of ancient Greece and Rome. It glorifies man and temporal things instead of God and eternal things, and it fosters secularization of society. *The Northern or Teutonic Renaissance* (primarily in Germany) focuses on rediscovering the knowledge of ancient Judaism and Christianity. It emphasizes the study of biblical manuscripts in Hebrew and Greek. The Gutenberg Bible, the first book produced with movable type, is printed in 1455 or 56. Erasmus publishes a Greek New Testament in 1516.

The Fall of Constantinople. In 1453 Constantinople and the Eastern Roman Empire (Byzantium) fall to the Muslim Turks. Thus the Eastern Orthodox Church stagnates and grows little.

Modern
Church History

THE REFORMATION CHURCH
(1517–1648)

*T*he Reformation in Germany. Martin Luther, an Augustinian monk, begins the Reformation in Germany in 1517. In 1529 Roman Catholic leaders and the emperor of the Holy Roman Empire decree Roman Catholicism the sole faith permitted in the empire. The political rulers of northern Germany favor Luther and protest. As a result, they are called *Protestants*. The Reformation in Germany gives birth to the Lutheran Church. Denmark, Norway, and Sweden adopt the Lutheran faith.

The Reformation in Switzerland. In northern Switzerland, Ulrich Zwingli, a Roman Catholic priest, establishes the Reformation in the cantons of Zurich and Bern in the 1520s. This begins the Reformed Church. In southern Switzerland, John Calvin, a French Protestant, organizes the Reformation in Geneva in the 1530s and 1540s, producing the Presbyterian Church.

The Reformation in England. From the 1530s to 1550s King Henry VIII severs the Church of England from the Roman Catholic Church organizationally, and King Edward VI severs it theologically. This spawns the Anglican Church.

The Reformation in Scotland. From the 1550s to 1560s John Knox leads a group of committed nobles to establish the Presbyterian Church in Scotland.

The Reformation in France. In the 1520s Jacques Lefevre establishes the Reformed Church in France. By 1560 almost one-sixth of all French people are Protestant and are known as *Huguenots*.

The Reformation in the Netherlands. Until 1525 most Protestants in the Netherlands are Lutheran; from 1525 to 1540 the Anabaptists (later known as *Mennonites*) are predominant; from 1540 on, the Reformed Church becomes predominant.

The Anabaptists. Conrad Grebel launches the Anabaptist movement in Switzerland. The key Anabaptist in Germany is Balthasar Hubmaier; in the Netherlands, it is Menno Simons. Unlike other reformers, the Anabaptists are pacifists. They insist on believer's baptism, complete separation of church and state, and a church of believers only.

Reformation Truths. The Reformation emphasizes three major New Testament truths: justification by faith alone, the priesthood of every believer, and the Bible alone as the final authority for faith and practice.

The Counter-Reformation. To prevent Europe from becoming totally Protestant, the Roman Catholic Church establishes the Jesuit Order in 1534 to fight heresy and spread Roman Catholicism by missionary activity. Through radical means, it wins back significant areas and people to Rome. The church uses government military force and reinstitutes the Inquisition in 1542. Thousands of Protestants are tortured, killed, or forced to recant their Protestant beliefs. In 1543 the Index, a list

of books that Catholics are forbidden to read under threat of judgment, is published. From 1545 to 1563 the Council of Trent meets and makes the following pronouncements: The Apocrypha is canonical Scripture; the Bible, Apocrypha, and church tradition are equal and are the final authority for faith and practice; only the Roman Catholic Church can interpret these things; justification is by faith plus works; salvation comes only through sacraments administered by Roman Catholic priests; only ordained clergy are priests; the body and blood of Christ are in the bread of the Mass, so the laity doesn't need the cup. This council made the idea of apostolic succession official dogma.

The Thirty Years War. From 1618 to 1648 Catholic and Protestant forces war against each other. Germany loses nearly one-third of its population. With the peace treaty in 1648, most religious persecution ends. Holland and

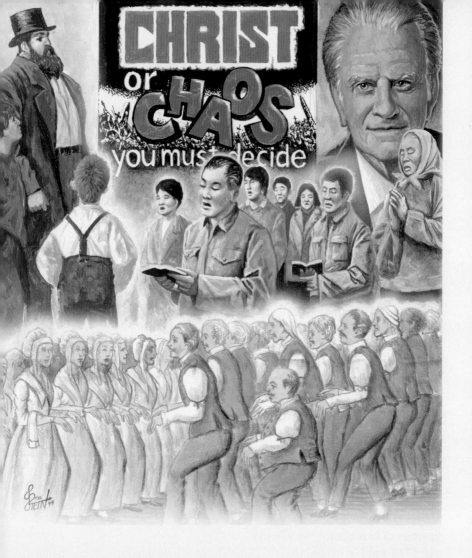

Switzerland are recognized as independent Protestant states. Lutheranism and Calvinism become recognized religions in Germany. Protestants receive the right to hold offices in Roman Catholic governments. France becomes the dominant power in Europe.

THE EXPANDING CHURCH (1648–1800)

Christianity Comes to America. The *Anglican Church* becomes the state church of Virginia in 1607 and later of New York, Maryland, South Carolina, Georgia, and North Carolina. It is the dominant, English colonial church until the American Revolution. In the 1600s English Puritans establish the *Congregational Church* in Massachusetts, Connecticut, and parts of Rhode Island.

In the 1600s the *Baptist Church* emerges in parts of Rhode Island, then New Hampshire in the 1700s. From the 1500s to the mid-1700s, *Roman Catholicism* is the predominant faith in North America; but when England takes North America from France in the French and Indian War, Protestantism becomes predominant. The *Reformed Church* is the state church of New Netherlands until England takes that colony from the Dutch in 1664, renaming it New York and making the Anglican Church the state church. *Lutheran Churches* are founded in New Amsterdam and Delaware in the 1600s. In the 1700s many *Quakers, Mennonites, Moravians,* and *Lutherans* come to Pennsylvania because that colony establishes complete religious freedom for all faiths. In the first half of the 1700s, some 100,000 *Presbyterians* of Scottish descent migrate from Northern Ireland to New York, New Jersey, Pennsylvania, and Virginia. The *Methodist Church* arrives in the late 1700s.

Enemies of Christianity. Between 1648 and 1789 a new system of thought called *Rationalism* develops. It maintains that man does not need divine revelation and can know everything through human senses, reason, and scientific research. Rationalism spawns a religion of reason called *Deism.* Deism contends that after God created the universe, He withdrew from it to let it be governed solely by natural law. It rejects all these: the Bible as divine revelation to mankind, the deity of Jesus Christ, all miracles and prophecies, and the sinful nature of man. It claims that man is basically good and perfectible and capable of producing a perfect order on earth. Deism begins in England, then spreads to France, Germany, and America. Rationalism and Deism lay the foundation for destructive criticism and liberal theology.

Revivalism. Revivalism stresses a vital, personal religious experience and practical Christian living. Various expressions of it develop in several locations simultaneously. *Pietism* begins in Germany as an evangelical attempt to correct the

dead orthodoxy of 17th-century Lutheranism. The Moravian Church begins as an outgrowth of Pietism in the 1700s, and it sends missionaries to the West Indies, Greenland, and Africa. The *Wesleyan Revivals* of the 1700s help transform England from moral and drunken debauchery and revolution to a leader of nations and keeper of world peace during the 19th century. It gives birth to the Methodist Church and encourages the beginning of the Sunday school movement. The *Great Awakening* of the 1700s turns the American colonies away from moral and religious decline. Presbyterian, Baptist, Methodist, and some Reformed preachers take part in this spiritual awakening. Thousands become true followers of Christ; hundreds of new churches, several new colleges, missionary endeavors, and humanitarian works emerge.

The Churches and the American Revolution. The Congregationalists, Baptists, and Presbyterians support the Revolution zealously. The Quakers, Mennonites, and Moravians are pacifists and support neither side. The Methodists try to remain neutral but are accused of favoring England because John Wesley supports the king. The Anglicans support the Revolution in the south, are evenly divided in the Mid-Atlantic colonies, and support England in New England. Because Anglican support of England becomes a stigma, after the Revolution the Anglican Church in America changes its name to the Protestant Episcopal Church.

THE NINETEENTH-CENTURY CHURCH (1800–1900 A.D.)

Christianity in England. Several distinct movements in the 19th century characterize the Anglican Church. The Evangelical Movement produces outstanding pastors, Bible scholars, hymn writers, social reformers, and tract and missionary societies. The Broad Church Movement promotes the social gospel and liberal theology. The Oxford Movement emphasizes ritual and organization and is like the Roman Catholic Church, except it rejects the authority of the pope. The *Nonconformists*—Protestants outside the Anglican Church—include the Brethren, which begins in Dublin, Ireland, around 1830; the Young Men's Christian Association, which arises in 1844; and the Salvation Army in 1878. The *English Protestant Missionary* effort begins in 1792 as a result of the vision of William Carey. The Baptists, Congregationalists, Presbyterians, Anglican evangelicals, and Methodists form missionary societies.

Enemies of Historic, Biblical Christianity. During the late 1700s and 1800s several philosophies systematically undermine historic, biblical Christianity and lay the foundation for liberal theology. Immanuel Kant asserts that man can know God exists only through man's sense of moral obligation. George W. F. Hegel denies all absolutes except the state. Friedrich Schleiermacher contends that personal, subjective experience is ultimate authority. Karl Marx propagates atheistic communism; Charles Darwin, evolution; Soren Kierkegaard, existentialism; and Sigmund Freud, psychoanalysis. Destructive biblical criticism develops. All these deny objective, historic revelation from God to mankind and claim the Bible cannot be divinely inspired revelation.

Liberal Theology. Liberal theology is open to all viewpoints except biblical Christianity. It believes that science can lead to all truth and is skeptical concerning the possibility of achieving absolute knowledge of ultimate reality. It emphasizes similarities rather than differences between Christianity and other religions, the supernatural and natural, God and man, the church and the world. It believes in man's inherent goodness and perfectibility and in subjective religious experience as authority. It emphasizes Jesus Christ as the greatest teacher and example of morality and ethics but denies His deity, substitutionary atonement, and bodily resurrection. It proclaims a God of love, devoid of wrath or judgment, and a gospel of societal redemption from social wrongs, not personal redemption from sin. During the 1800s many colleges, seminaries, and church groups defect from historic, biblical Christianity to liberal theology.

Christianity in America. In the late 1700s and early 1800s, a *Second Awakening* comes first to American colleges, then spreads to frontier areas in the form of camp meetings. It gives rise to midweek prayer meetings and prompts the formation of the following: denominational home, foreign, and black missionary societies; new theological seminaries and church colleges; Protestant parochial schools; a national Sunday school movement; Bible and tract societies; and religious journals. During the 1800s America also experiences the Finney revivals; the rise of liberal Unitarian and Universalist Church movements; the formation of several new denominations; the beginnings of Mormonism, Seventh-Day Adventism, Spiritualism, Christian Science, and Jehovah's Witnesses; the founding of crusades for temperance, Sabbath observance, and abolition of slavery; the beginnings of city rescue missions, America's Young Men's Christian Association (Y.M.C.A.),

Young Women's Christian Association, and Salvation Army; the Dwight. L. Moody revivals; the beginnings of the Bible school movement, evangelical faith mission boards, and Bible and prophecy conferences.

THE TWENTIETH-CENTURY CHURCH (1900-2000 A.D.)

The Modernist-Fundamentalist Controversy. The extensive spread of liberal theology draws strong reactions from theological conservatives. In 1909 a set of scholarly volumes, *The Fundamentals*, defend the doctrines of historic, biblical Christianity. In 1919 the World's Christian Fundamentals Association is founded to combat modernist (liberal) teaching. Major controversies between modernists and fundamentalists within denominations prompt many people to separate and form new, conservative denominations and fellowships.

European Theology. After World War I a new theological movement, Neo Orthodoxy, begins a revolt in Western Europe against liberal theology. Contrary to liberal theology, it stresses the sinfulness of man and the difference between God and the universe. But contrary to orthodoxy, it injects a destructive, critical view of the Bible and claims that God has not given revelation in the form of declared statements of truth. By the late 1940s Neo Orthodoxy dominates most European and American theological schools. But after the 1960s European theology falls into such chaos that some scholars fear Protestantism may end in Europe.

The Ecumenical Movement. This movement promotes unity through these means: interdenominational cooperation, union of denominations, national federations of church groups, international councils and fellowships, dialogues between groups within Christendom and between Christendom and non-Christian religions, Catholic observers at World Council of Churches' meetings, Protestant observers at Roman Catholic meetings, and joint participation in large public rallies. Most efforts negate the importance of doctrinal truth in favor of unity. Some support radical, left-wing groups.

Roman Catholicism. In 1950 Pope Pius XII proclaims the bodily assumption of Mary to heaven after her death. Vatican II Council (1962-1965) encourages Catholics to read the Bible, asserts spiritual priesthood for the laity, permits the Mass to be conducted in the language of each nation, and exhibits an ecumenical spirit toward Protestantism and Eastern Orthodoxy. The tendency grows to regard Mary as co-redemptrix with Christ.

Neo-Evangelicalism. By the late 1940s a new movement begins in conservative circles to enable orthodoxy to impact the world and be respected by it. The movement develops these characteristics: increased emphasis on scholarship, a willingness to re-examine and modify doctrinal beliefs to fit the modern mind, a tendency to interpret the Bible in light of science, a desire to share theological insights with liberal and neo-orthodox thinkers, ecumenical evangelism, a tendency to minimize the importance of doctrine and biblical eschatology, a strategy to infiltrate liberal denominations (rather than separate from them) to win them back to orthodoxy, and an attempt to develop a social philosophy.

Pentecostalism and the Charismatic Movement. Early in the 1900s the Pentecostal movement arises, emphasizing tongues and other apostolic-age sign and revelational gifts. Pentecostal denominations arise. In the 1960s this emphasis enters mainline Protestant churches, the Roman Catholic Church, and spawns the charismatic movement. Because it stresses experiences common to people, of varying church backgrounds, it plays a key role in the spirit of ecumenicity.